Other books by Author

WW I   The Battle Of The MInd

WW II   This My Cell

WW III   Scars And Memories

WW IV   Voices

WW V   Alone I Roam

WW VI   2020 Deepend

WW VII   Seven

WW VIII   My Mental State

... more will be revealed soon...

WAR WITHIN

WW VI:
2020, Deep End

VOLUME 6 OF 7

MICHAEL R. BANE

WestBow
P R E S S®
A DIVISION OF THOMAS NELSON
& ZONDERVAN

WestBow Press books may be ordered through booksellers or by contacting:

WestBow Press
A Division of Thomas Nelson & Zondervan
1663 Liberty Drive
Bloomington, IN 47403
www.westbowpress.com
844-714-3454

All Scripture quotations are taken from the King James Version.

ISBN: 978-1-6642-3650-9 (sc)
ISBN: 978-1-6642-3651-6 (e)

Print information available on the last page.

WestBow Press rev. date: 06/22/2021

CONTENTS

Chapter 1 You Lose

When It Was Written.. 1

Watch Me Burn 2

Really... 4

Speck of Sand... 5

I Won't Be Quiet.. 6

You Can't Hide 7

Me, My Murderer 8

Chapter 2 My Armor

When It Was Written..13

This Armor...14

Faith 15

Therefore, I Win...16

I Belong 18

House of Flies 19

Let Me Go 20

Battle of the Mind..21

Chapter 3 Written Words

When It Was Written..25

Writers Past 26

It Is Finished 28

A Letter.. 29

Your Story 30

Diary of Shame 32

My Words 33

This Ink 34

Chapter 4   You, My Enemy

When It Was Written 39
So Close 40
Perfect Imperfection 42
This Part of Me 43
My Seething... 44
Tormenting Conflicts 45
Day After Day... 46
Loves Nothing 47

Chapter 5   Me, Not Mine

When It Was Written 51
Have You Ever?...52
A War On Everything 53
Little Hole 54
Not Mine 55
Show Me, You 56
Slowly Kills Me 57
Its Me, Its Not..58
Talkin to Myself 59

Chapter 6   Deceived

When It Was Written 63
Familiar 64
Wisper..65
A World Full 66
Chasing Monsters..67
You Can't Hide 68
Double Standards..69

Chapter 7 Trickery

When It Was Written...73

Ponder On This..74

Crawl...75

Evil Empire..76

Their Face 77

No Compromise...78

Murder Now 79

All Is Not...80

DEDICATION

2020 – Deep End –

I dedicate this WW VI to you, my
Sister Crystal.
How many discussions, and cups of coffee
we had during this insane year.
We share so many beliefs. I learned so
much from you this year.
Balancing politics with my core beliefs
is not the easiest thing to do.
Through all of our talks, I was kinda
able to do it. And for that, I thank you.
And for so much more.
Your strength keeps people alive.

INTRO WWVI

2020 – Deep End –

Everything within these pages was written
in the year 2020. These "unprecedented times".
Like all my writings, there are multiple
messages, within, throughout.
My hopes are that, we all will see, and also
think about everything that is going on.
These maybe "unprecedented times", but
do not be fooled. Do not be tricked, by
everything that's going on.
It was all written, and
God is still in control.

CHAPTER 1

YOU LOSE

Luke 9:25

For what is a man advantaged, if he gain the whole
world and lose himself or be cast away?

KJV

WHEN IT WAS WRITTEN

I -   Watch Me Burn, 2020

II -   Really, 2020

III - Speck of Sand, 2020

IV - I Won't Be Quiet, 2020

V -   You Can't Hide, 2020

VI - Me, My Monster, 2020

WATCH ME BURN

So glad I didn't get
what I deserve

Grace, the favor, I
didn't earn

Because the enemy, he
wants to watch me burn

His lies his deceit, a
new trap at every turn

The scales, they fell
from my eyes

And, I saw my Lord
take my place

I will not get
what I deserve

The gift, I
did not earn

This favor, I can
never return

The enemy cannot
touch me

Though he wants to
watch me burn

A new snare, at
every turn

The scales, they
fell from my eyes

The gift I did
not earn

I will not get
what I deserve

And, he will not get to
watch me burn -

REALLY

It's time to go back
a few years later
no one really knows

So let's fast forward
to a time before
nothing really matters

So time is time
when all stands still
and space doesn't really exist

It's only where I am
and where you were
neither, neither really care

As weather height, or depth
sight, or sounds
nothing really matters

Its space versus time
both win, both lose
No one really knows –

SPECK OF SAND

How about getting off that
high horse you're riding

How about getting your
head out of the sky

How about getting your
feet on the ground

How about seeing
its bigger than you

How about your spirit
How about your soul

Where does it come from?
And where does it go?

How about seeing
its bigger than you

Your just one speck of sand
And, I'm one speck to ...

I WON'T BE QUIET

We're not surprised
I won't be quiet
thank-you, you're welcome –

We're not your puppets
I won't be quiet
we will not succumb –

We're not afraid
I won't be quiet
we will overcome –

YOU CAN'T HIDE

So much wrong
I need to help
to make it right

So much darkness
I need to help
to bring some light

So much violence
So much hate

Where does it
go from here?

So much deception
So many lies

You can't hide forever
in your darkness

I need to help
to bring you to the light

ME, MY MURDERER

So many people cry
So many people die
This is war
Me, my murderer
I kill myself by my mistakes
by the drugs, I take
It was not always
this way.
I am to blame.
This is a war, I cannot win
I kill myself
Me, my murderer
So many people die
So many people cry
If you are not like me,
you can not understand these things

But you can understand
the lives it changed
And the pain it brings
by my mistakes
by the drugs, I take
So many lives changed
So many families rearranged
If you are not like me
you can not understand such things
But, you can understand
the pain it brings
By my mistakes
By the drugs, I take
I kill myself
Me, my murderer
So many people cry ...

CHAPTER 2

MY ARMOR

Ephesians 6:11

Put on the whole armour of God, that ye may be able
to stand against the wiles of the devil.

KJV

WHEN IT WAS WRITTEN

I -   This Armor, 2020

II -   Faith, 2020

III -   Therefore, I Win, 2020

IV -   I Belong, 2020

V -   House of Flies, 2020

VI -   Let Me Go, 2020

VII -   Battle of the Mind, 2020

THIS ARMOR

One of those days
became one of those years
I woke up today
listening to your lies
trying to spread fear.
This is war, but
the battle is not real.
Its just another
one of those days
that became another
one of those years.
Although, it may seem different
its really not
it was all written
you can not penetrate
this armor ...
spew your lies
spread your fear
I woke up today
ready for you. LOL ...

FAITH

Faith is more than facing death
Faith is also about embracing life

Where faith exists
There is no fear

Faith is more than facing life
Its also about embracing death

Faith is there to heal the past
Faith is there to face the future

Faith is always there
If you ever need it

Fear cannot exist
When faith is there ...

THEREFORE, I WIN

I know what its like to be
judged on my appearance
as they roll their eyes
or shake their heads

But it helps me not to judge
those who cross my path
and see that they are exactly
where they are supposed to be
at this moment, and
so therefore, I win ...

I know what its like to be
locked in a cage, and wait,
and hope that someone
will bring me the key

But, it helps me to enjoy my
Freedom, and to be able to
acknowledge, what it is
to be truly free, and
so therefore, I win ...

I know what it is like to be
doubted, and to be
considered not good enough

But, it helps me to root
For the underdog, and to
Search for the best in others,
and to also help them to
See it in themselves, and
So therefore, I win ...

I know what it is like to
be on the wrong side of
the tracks, where nobody
wants you to cross

But it helps me to feel
everyone's pain, and
so therefore, I win ...

I know what its like to
accept me, and to love me
so therefore, I win ...

I BELONG

I sometimes worry that,
I don't know where to go
Not sure where I belong

I sometimes worry that
I'm a mistake,
I'm doing wrong

I sometimes worry that
I won't last, that
this life is too long

I sometimes worry that
I am week, but I
remember, He is strong

I sometimes worry
then I remember,
to whom, I belong

HOUSE OF FLIES

You can not touch me
You are still alive
in the house of flies

You will get others
but me, no, I will not be
in the house of flies

You do not own me
but, you still thrive
in the house of flies

You can not win
though, you will survive
in your house of flies

LET ME GO

Lift me up
or let me go

Will you lift me up
to just let me go?

If you are gonna
lift me up
to just let me go

Just go
just let me go

BATTLE OF THE MIND

Your weapons from below
cannot penetrate my
armor from above
your weapons
of hate, doubt, and fear
my armor
of love, faith, and strength
your weapons from below
my armor from above
I'm ready for you
I'm prepared for your kind
your weapons
my armor
the battle of the mind –

CHAPTER 3

WRITTEN WORDS

Job 19:23

Oh that my words were now written!
Oh that they were printed in a book.

KJV

WHEN IT WAS WRITTEN

I -   Writers Past, 2020

II -   It Is Finished, 2020

III - A Letter, 2020

IV -   Your Story, 2020

V -   Diary of Shame, 2020

VI -   My Words, 2020

VII - This Ink, 2020

WRITERS PAST

There is something strange
that I will attempt to explain
When I am all alone
and there is nobody there
and I know that I'm certain
that nobody cares
Its always my pen, and
It helps me to see
that he is my friend
when their is no one there
and their is nowhere to turn
my pen is there, to help me to mend.
Its hard to explain, and
harder to understand
But someone else takes over, and
puts the pen in my hand
is it possibly from writers past?

Is it a continuous flow of ink
that will always last?
The more answers I get
the more questions I ask ...
So as I try to explain
From where this power came
My pen brings me back to me
it reminds me to look
and it helps me to see
that I am never alone
The ink flows through me
From my heart to my head
with my blood, through my veins
it helps me to put
my pain on, the page
my pen help me not to
dig my own grave ...

IT IS FINISHED

The battle within is real
The Holy Spirit is at
war with my flesh –
And I lose plenty of
the battles
But I will not
lose the war –
I cannot lose the war –
It was all
nailed to the cross –
and when He said
IT IS FINISHED
– I won ... –

A LETTER

If my life was a letter
that anyone could read
by simply looking at me.

How would this letter read?
If anyone could see
and simply watch me.

Things that are not
written on paper,
or even etched in stone.

But the things that I do
on a daily basis
if anyone could see this.

Now, how would it read?
not with ink, or words
But with God's living spirit.

If my life was a letter
is it something, that even I
would want to read?

YOUR STORY

Everyone has a thought
I'd love to hear your story
of your memories
and of your life
As, I write mine on paper
it makes me think of you
so many thoughts
so many memories
If I could see through
your mind's eye
To understand your story
your memories of your life
what makes you, you
who you are
It separates you, from all.
But also keeps us connected
so many memories
so many thoughts
as days turn to years
now decades, their gone
your story, remains
Don't take it with you,
it must be told ...

As only you can tell it.
We may share many memories
But the ones you keep
they are you
Some of them you may
have let go of.
Of those you hold
only you know.

If I could see through
your mind's eye
to understand your story
what makes you, you
who you are
How you got here
How you got through
As I write mine on paper
and I think of you
So many thoughts
so many memories
If I could see through
your mind's eye
your story remains
do not take it with you
It must be told ...

DIARY OF SHAME

I won't look away
as you write in your
diary of shame.
Writing your lies
talking about change
same story
just rearranged
your thoughts and reasons.
are deranged
I won't look away
as you try to explain
when its all written
in your diary of shame.

MY WORDS

When you see me
I want you to feel me

When you read my words
I need you to know me

I am not only me
I am also you

When I see you
I also see me

When you read my words
I need you, to see me

But more importantly
I need you, to know you

THIS INK

I took a journey through my mind
so many memories
are there to find

To some I run to
from others, I flee
I want to use my experiences
to help someone like me

I want to change this world
with my paper, and my pen
So this ink spills
from many places I have been

Their are times I don't
wanna do this anymore
But I put my pen to paper
and I'm not sure who its for

If I stop writing
I may just die
So the truth must be told
to defeat the lie
that you are not worth it

I'm here to say you are
and so am I.

So this ink continues
to flow
Is it for you,
or is it for me?

Only the ink knows ...

CHAPTER 4

YOU, MY ENEMY

Psalms 119:98

Thou through thy commandments hast made me wiser
than mine enemies, for they are ever with me.

KJV

WHEN IT WAS WRITTEN

I -   So Close, 2020

III -   Perfect Imperfection, 2020

IV -   This Part of Me, 2020

V -   My Seething, 2020

VI -   Tormenting Conflicts, 2020

VII -   Day After Day, 2020

VIII - Loves Nothing, 2020

SO CLOSE

So close, but yet so far away
as if I could reach out
and touch, and smell
the wantness of your breath
or taste the sweetness of your lips
so close, but yet
you are not here
I'm not really sure how
to go on without you near
So, I drive myself insane
why is everything so heavy?
So close, but yet so far
If I could just let go
of the thought of you, and
the sweetness of your breath
saw a saint in side of me

You wanna know if I'm
a friend, or enemy

My angels, and my demons
they don't know their place

Not really sure which one
will come out and play

and this is a part of me

Without the darkness
there would be no light in me

Ready or not
I wanna come out and play.

PERFECT IMPERFECTION

Perfect imperfection
is there really such a thing?

How can something so terrible
be so good for me?

And why is it when I look at you
the truth I cannot see?

I try to see the best in you
you bring out the worst in me

Why is something I know is wrong
what it is I think I need?

Perfect imperfection
nothings what it seems

Regardless if its right or wrong
I feel you, are what I need

THIS PART OF ME

Something take this part of me
Something breaks this heart in me
You, and I were meant to be
I feel you were sent to me

So, why do you break this heart in me?
Why do you take this part of me?
This is not how its suppose to be
You, and I were meant to be

As insane as all this seems
Your whispers, become my screams
I feel you were sent to me
to take this part of me

Is this how its meant to be?
For you to break this heart in me?
Were you really sent to me,
to take this part of me?

MY SEETHING

My rage you are feeding
My torn heart is bleeding
So much hurt, my seething
I'm barely breathing
I say nothing, but
inside I'm screaming
Now I'm believing
because of you
My torn heart is bleeding
My rage, my seething

TORMENTING CONFLICTS

Broken pieces
but, not torn apart
tormenting conflicts
ripped out my heart
mental defects
physical aspects
social rejects
Broken in pieces
but, not torn apart

DAY AFTER DAY

Why you try to drive me insane?
Your same confusion
Its just your way
Spewing your venum
day after day ...
My phone rings, its you
trying to drive me insane
The devils calling, its you
its just your way
your same confusion
day after day ...

LOVES NOTHING

Beautiful, is ugly
You're beautiful it seems
Beautiful, loves no one
You're beautiful, a dream

Beautiful, is empty
You're beautiful, no cares
Beautiful, loves nothing
You're beautiful, a nightmare

CHAPTER 5

ME, NOT MINE

Ezekiel 2:10

And he spread it before me; and it was written within and without: And
there was written therein lamentations, and morning, and woe.

KJV

WHEN IT WAS WRITTEN

I -   Have You Ever?..., 2020

II -   A War On Everything, 2020

III -   Little Hole, 2020

IV -   Not Mine, 2020

V -   Show Me, You..., 2020

VI -   Slowly Kills Me, 2020

VII -   Its Me, Its Not, 2020

VIII -   Talkin to Myself, 2020

HAVE YOU EVER?..

Have you ever touched someone
and everything else just disappeared?

Have you ever thought of loosing someone
and got scared?

Have you ever loved someone so deep?
have you ever needed someone
you knew you couldn't keep?

Have you ever kissed someone
and forgot to breathe?

Have you ever looked in someone's eyes
and just believed?

A WAR ON EVERYTHING

The war within
a war on everything ...

Everything you used to know
everything you used to be.

A war on everything
the war within, misery.

Forget all you used to know
you're not who you used to be.

The war within
A war on everything ...

The battle is real
Say good-bye
to all you used to be ...

LITTLE HOLE

I was whole
But, when you left
you took a piece of me
you left a little hole

That hole it grows
its more of you
there is less of me
I was whole

If you look at me
and can't see me
you probably see that hole

It started out so small
when you left
But, that hole it grows

If you look at me
and can't see me
please, help me fill that hole

NOT MINE

Cleanse the hate
from deep within
wash the sorrow
from off my skin
Time to clear my path
stop living in the past
I need a reason –
so much pain, I retain
and its not even mine ...
wash the sorrow
From off my skin
that seeps from deep within
so much I retain
that's not even mine ...
I need a reason –

SHOW ME, YOU ...

Your mask cannot hide
the real you

Your make-up cannot
change the ugly
that you do.

So take off your mask
shows me, you ...

Remove your make-up
and show me

How beautiful
you truly are

Show me, you ...

SLOWLY KILLS ME

Look right through me
You look right through me
Why can't you see me?
It hurts more
than you can believe
It hurts so much more
You can't conceive
What it does to me
When you look right through me
It slowly kills me.
Look right through me

ITS ME, ITS NOT

I should be fine
but I'm not
Is this mind mine?
It is, but its not ...
Something comes over me
not me, not myself
I should be fine
but I'm not
please help me separate
this, my mind
Its me, but its not ...

TALKIN TO MYSELF

I'm talkin to myself
and I don't know
what to say ...
I rarely have this problem
but everything just seems
so different today.
I'm talkin to myself
and I can't hear
what I say ...
my mind is unclear
and cluttered with all
that's going on today.

I'm talkin to myself
and I can finally
hear what I say ...
my mind is now open
and its my choice to choose
If I listen, or hear
to everything that's
going on today ...

CHAPTER 6

DECEIVED

Ephesians 5:6a

Let no man deceive you with vain words;

KJV

WHEN IT WAS WRITTEN

I -   Familiar, 2020

II -   Wisper, 2020

III -   A World Full, 2020

IV -   Chasing Monsters, 2020

V -   You Can't Hide, 2020

VI -   Double Standards, 2020

FAMILIAR

I'm a believer
I need a savior
not a deceiver

I can feel you there
are you a lie?
or do you care?

Are you my savior?
or my deceiver?

Your voice sounds familiar
but your messages
are not similar

I can feel you near
you are both here

My savior
and my deceiver

WISPER

I'm trying to see your face
I'm trying to find my place
I'm trying to share your space
trying not to leave a trace
You're trying not to hurry
I'm trying to win this race
You're trying to see Gods glory
I'm trying to seek His grace

You're trying to stay the same
I'm trying to change
You probably shouldn't of came
I'm trying to change your name
I'm trying to find my place

I'm trying to wake from this nightmare
You're trying to live a dream
I'm trying to whisper
You're trying to scream
You probably shouldn't of come here
Its probably too late for you to leave
My nightmare, your dream ...

A WORLD FULL

A world full
of empty spaces
deep, dark places
and ugly faces
people deceived
they believe their own lies
those types
are the worst kind
spreading propaganda
from their twisted
little minds
A world full
of crazy double standards
they worry about issues
that don't really matter
please don't be duped
they hate
they are loathing
stay clear
they are monsters
they are wolves
in sheep's clothing –

CHASING MONSTERS

Sometimes looking for love
is the same as
chasing monsters

Sometimes chasing a dream
is often an illusion

She may have outward beauty
but inside
she is a monster.

So is it her you're looking for?
or are you
chasing monsters?

YOU CAN'T HIDE

So much wrong
I need to help to
make it right

So much darkness
I need to help to
bring some light

So much violence
So much hate

Where does it go
From here?

So much deception
So many lies

You can't hide forever
in your darkness

I need to help to
bring you to the light.

DOUBLE STANDARDS

Warped by confusion
duped by delusion
your government –
raped by intrusion
trapped by illusion
your religion –
you have your rights
but, I don't have mine
your double standards –
your lies, and manipulation
spreading your fear
you can not touch me –
you can not change me –
right is right
wrong is wrong

CHAPTER 7

TRICKERY

Ephesians 6:12

For we wrestle not against flesh and blood, but against
principalities, against powers, against the rulers of the darkness of
this world. Against spiritual wickedness in high places.

KJV

WHEN IT WAS WRITTEN

I -   Ponder On This, 2020

II -   Crawl, 2020

III -   Evil Empire, 2020

V -   Their Face, 2020

VI -   No Compromise, 2020

VII -   Murder Now, 2020

VIII - All Is Not, 2020

PONDER ON THIS

We have all heard the story
of the wolf in sheep's clothing

But what about the sheep
who is in wolves clothing?

Pause for a moment, and
ponder on this notion

Can you make sense of
this sentiment?

The wolf in sheep's clothing
is out to deceive

But the sheep in wolves clothing
can not be deceived.

So, your trickery
will not work on me.

For, I am His sheep
ponder on this a moment ...

CRAWL

You may attempt
to infiltrate
But you cannot
come within
you may creep
into my mind
But you cannot
crawl
in my skin

EVIL EMPIRE

This is not my home
evil empire
This is not where I belong

I'll tell you through my story
you'll read it in the psalms

This is not a surprise
evil empire
It was told ages ago

The truth must be told
The prophecies of old

This is not my home
evil empire

THEIR FACE

Regardless what you think
No matter what they say
I think they are out to get me –

They never disappear
I always see their face
Regardless of what they think
no matter what you say
I know they are out to get me –

They will never stop searching
there is nowhere that I'm safe
they never go away
I always see their face –

No matter what you say
No matter what they think
at some point
at some place
I know they are gonna get me –

NO COMPROMISE

You don't need to lie
We don't need to die
No surprise
No compromise
Straight out lies
They won't work
All your tries
We don't need to die
You don't need to lie
No surprise
No compromise

MURDER NOW

Will you be the death of me?
I look at you
But, you are not what I see
Murder now, is that
What will be?

Why will you be the
death of me?
Murder now, is what I see
I look at you, and
wonder what will be –

Will I allow you to be the
death of me?
Murder now, it will not be
I look at you,
and its you, I see –

ALL IS NOT

All is not lost ...
I will not give up
I will not fall
I will not bow,
Only to my Lord

All is not what it seems ...
I will not bend
I will not break
I will not bow,
Only to my Lord

All is not real ...
I will not be afraid
I will not kneel
I will not bow,
Only to my Lord

Printed in the United States
by Baker & Taylor Publisher Services